September 2010
ferry from Munkuliet
to Jersey

My Nantucket Boyhood

Francis W. Pease

This book is dedicated to my very patient wife, Mary, and also to Mary Miles for her editing help and urging me to complete the story.

Copyright © 2004 by Francis W. Pease
Book Design by Melody Olbrych

All rights reserved. No part of this book may be reproduced or transmitted in any form by any means, electronic or mechanical, including photocopying and recording, or by any storage and retrieval system without permission in writing from the publisher.

ISBN 1-59457-479-0

BookSurge, LLC
North Charleston, SC
Library of Congress Control Number: 2004107366

1 2 3 4 5

Manufactured in the United States of America
Cover photo of the Easy Street Basin courtesy of the Nantucket Historical Association

My Nantucket Boyhood

Francis W. Pease

Having had the good fortune to be born on Nantucket Island on March 20, 1923, I have tried hard to spend most of my life here. I was told that I was born in the wee small hours of the morning in the midst of a northeast blizzard, in the old Nantucket Cottage Hospital on West Chester Street. My source of information on that subject was the lady in charge of the entire production. All the houses that comprised that hospital are still standing as private homes, but no longer connected.

The best thing I can say about my childhood is "so far, so good." My generation came along in the deep dark days of the infamous Depression. But I always felt, and still do, that if one had to grow up in those years there was no better place to do it than Nantucket. Because it was a summer resort, there was always some, even if only a little, money to be earned. It wasn't always easy for a kid to earn money, but it could be done. We lived at 19 Hussey Street, and there was a sizable lot of land with the old (1758) house. My parents raised a lot of our vegetables, and I was allowed an area in which to raise my own. Later on I would fill my little wooden wagon with vegetables and sell them door-to-door. It worked pretty well; I earned enough to finally buy my first bicycle, which I kept and used almost daily right up to World War II. I also managed to buy a twelve-foot skiff a couple of years after the purchase of the bike, and it was my own private luxury yacht. When I first had it in the water I rowed it so much my back muscles were painfully sore, but I wouldn't quit and finally worked

I

out the cramps. I spent hundreds of hours all over Nantucket Harbor in that skiff, and was able to tie it up in the Easy Street basin, very often with the help and kindness of the Andrews brothers, Clinton and George, who always had time to help any youngster and show him helpful things about boating. I doubt if a skiff would last long now, unattended in Easy Street, or anywhere else in Nantucket today.

I used to love to row over to Coatue, dig some littlenecks, build a small fire on the beach, and cook myself a lunch of steamed clams. Tough but tasty, because I had cooked them myself. Another profitable venture was to use some of the quahogs for bait, tie up to the black can buoy in the middle of the harbor, catch some scup, and sell them to some of the people on boats moored in the harbor. Once in a while I would get employed as a water taxi, which also proved to be profitable. (Can't you imagine the "authorities" letting a kid get away with that now?) Once or twice I put my bike in the skiff and rowed over to Coatue to ride the outside beach, but that beach was softer and it was never as good as riding the north shore of Nantucket.

My skiff was only twelve feet long and very light, and therefore was a delight to row. As young men, in about 1949, my brother-in-law Byron Coffin and I beefed up the stern of that same boat, put a small outboard motor on it, and went scalloping in Madaket Harbor. I would think twice about doing anything like that now by myself, and I wouldn't even think of doing it two-handed. We did it quite safely and successfully, though. I still contend he could do just about anything with just about any boat.

The southeast corner of the steamboat wharf, and the rocks of the Old North Wharf, formed the basin of Easy Street, where I kept my skiff between Mr. Andrew's boathouse and the third boathouse, tied very cautiously.

— Photo courtesy of the
Nantucket Historical Association

One favorite stunt of two adventurous kids, myself and a chum, was to stand by at the southeast corner of the steamboat wharf and wait for the steamer Martha's Vineyard to arrive at 11:30 a.m. Just as it would poke its bow up to that corner and a crewman got a bowline to the dock, the steamer would start astern to back around to the north side of the wharf to unload. At that moment we would row hard, and the one in the bow of the skiff would grab hold of the bow of the Martha's Vineyard so that we would get a free ride to the north side of the wharf. We never got caught doing it. If my father had learned of it I'm sure he would have taken an axe to the skiff.

Part of the north side of the dock was open piling, and we used to like to be under it just as one of the steamers left. Here again, nobody would see us wiggling in there with the skiff, and just as the stern of the steamer would go by us we would push out into the propeller wash, and think we were shooting some rapids somewhere. Why we never swamped and had to swim, I don't know.

This same skiff was also used for duck hunting on Hummock Pond and Long Pond. My father and Mr. Winslow had a gunning camp on Long Pond, which was a good duck-shooting spot. My skiff got used for scalloping in Madaket Harbor for a very few seasons after World War II. It had been built of cedar by Mr. Emerson Chadwick, a very competent Nantucket carpenter. I remember drawing out $20 of my hard-earned savings to buy the skiff from him. I went right from the Savings Bank to Mr. Chadwick's house to minimize any danger of losing the small fortune I was carrying. He was very nice to me, and helped me get the skiff in tip-top condition, right next to his workshop, for a period of several days, due to my "work" schedule.

MAKING MONEY, FEATHERY FIGHTS

One stunt we used to indulge in to make money was collecting pint wine and whiskey bottles and selling them to Mr. Willard Hardy in the paint store, which was then located in one small storefront next to what is now the Atlantic Cafe. Mr. Hardy wanted the bottles for the purpose of selling small amounts of turpentine and linseed oil. He paid us two cents apiece and there were always some bottles to be found along the waterfront behind or under some of the fishing shanties. I used to be fascinated watching Mr. Hardy mixing lead putty in the back room. He could roll out a big gob of it and cut off one pound with precision. It seems like it is against the law to even mention the word "lead" now—how little the "environmentalists" really know about lead. Mr. Hardy also wanted us to produce cotton rags, but I couldn't do that because my father needed all he could get for cleaning and polishing the cars and the beach buses he ran in the summertime. More about those later.

In the late 1930's the world was moving toward a full-time war, and ships of United States registry had large American flags painted on their broadsides. Not to be outdone by any ocean-going vessel, I had to put flags on each side of my skiff. The "yachty" people seemed to enjoy that. (Anything for a laugh)

Another money-making venture was my magazine route. I proudly became the local agent for the weekly Saturday Evening Post, the monthly Ladies' Home Journal, and Country Gentleman, all Curtis Publishing Company publications. I hauled them around in my wagon until I graduated to a bike. A business was all well and good, but when it interfered with some other activity, such as sledding, skating, swimming, and so on, it was not so interesting.

The aforementioned little wooden wagon was the predecessor to my bike. Almost every kid my age had such a wagon, or something similar. We would kneel in one side of it and push with the other leg. I did that so much and for so long that I wore a hole through the wooden bed with the toe of my shoe. One's knee would get a little sore from the continuous kneeling on the bare wood, but an old pillow served to afford some relief. Roger Young lived in the neighborhood, and helped to keep things lively. His wagon was also equipped with a pillow. One day the two of us decided to have a pillow fight in Hussey Street near the rear entrance to Dr. and Mrs. Folger's property. In trying to kill each other in this manner, we succeeded only in breaking the pillows apart, thus scattering the feathers until the area looked like a summer snowstorm. We were nowhere to be seen when the local constabulary, having been summoned by Mrs. Folger, arrived on the scene.

STARTING SCHOOL WAY OFF-ISLAND

My education started in Florida, as my parents were spending winters there, allegedly to benefit my father's health, which it didn't do. I attended a little wooden country-style school, where I immediately fell in love with my first-grade teacher, Miss Ormsby, and I thought it was a great treat to spend a Saturday playing with her little brother, who was my age. I did well, but my downfalling was when my parents moved us all back north that spring, and I was placed in the first grade of Academy Hill School. It turned out to be a whole different affair, and I was the proverbial fish out of water. As a result, I did yet another year in the first grade, went on to the second grade in due form, and was then bounced to the fourth grade, and managed to make it the rest of the way in good order.

In St. Petersburg, I usually walked the mile home from the Clearview Avenue School; there was a paved road but very much countryside style, with practically no traffic. One day I was walking home alone and from the opposite direction came a unique sight—a very black man driving a mule and a two-wheeled wagon, heaped with fruit. When he got abreast of me he stopped, reached around behind himself, got two or three grapefruit and oranges, and tossed them down to me, all the time wearing a big grin. I stuffed them in my little lunchbox and proudly headed for home, not so afraid of the big black man any more.

On the way home from school it was necessary to cross a pair of railroad tracks, and in going up the tracks a short distance one would come to a large field where a farmer was raising sugar cane, among other things. The only thing we kids were interested in was the sugar cane, and we would liberate one or two stalks, go back to the road, and continue on our way home chewing on sugar cane. We never got caught at it— maybe it wasn't such a serious offense after all. This was probably 1928 or '29.

While spending one of our five winters in Florida, I became very sick with a colon infection, and very nearly didn't make it. Even as many years ago as that was, I can clearly remember having to learn to walk all over again, and how very shaky my legs were. During the recuperative time, my mother was obliged to strain any food I was allowed to eat, very much to my chagrin. Finally, when I was allowed to roam the neighborhood again, I immediately raided someone's vegetable garden and went home gnawing on a raw carrot, complete with dirt, which immediately horrified my mother. Thanks to her wonderful cooking, I survived, but was never overweight. My father claimed it was because I never sat in one place more than a minute.

I also contracted scarlet fever in Florida, which left its mark on my eyesight, and that caused me some inconvenience over the years, such as not being able to get into the Navy in World War II, and failing to get a government job I applied for after the war. But it didn't stop me from getting into the Army during the war, for what that was worth. At the time we graduated from high school, my friend and classmate Francis Perry was working for the local contingency of the U.S. Weather Bureau, but he couldn't get into any branch of the service during World War II because of his eyesight. I did manage to get into the Army, but after the war I couldn't get a job in the U.S. Weather Bureau because of my eyesight. So much for Uncle Sam's rationale. Incidentally, my getting into the Army made my father think the war wouldn't last more than another six months, as I had never held any job that long.

SUMMERS ON NANTUCKET

During the years my family traveled back and forth to Florida, we spent our Nantucket summers on Vestal Street, in a house owned by the Royal family. My father had three buses for the beach run, two Model-T Fords and one Reo, and of course two hired drivers. When we were five and six years old, we kids used to like to ride anywhere we could, and we would tease to ride downtown on one of the buses. We would be let off at the east end of Liberty Street, which was a two-way street in those years, as nearly all others were, and be told to walk directly home. We did walk directly home, but it was always through Howard Street, where there was a sizable barn complete with animals. On the east side of this barn was a pigpen, and we delighted in trying to converse with the pigs and otherwise get their attention. Clifton Cady was my usual companion on this venture. That barn was later converted into a house and named Greater Light, and is now a Nantucket Historical Association exhibit

I should tell you more about my father's Bathing Beach Bus Line. It ran from in front of the Atheneum to the Jetties and Cliffside Beaches, and it cost ten cents one way. Originally, the buses started out from alongside the old house that stood where the Post Office now stands. I was fairly popular with some of my contemporaries when it came to going to the beach, for obvious reasons. My father was very tolerant of this, and only required that we stay off the bus when it looked as if all the seats would be filled with paying passengers. When we graduated to bikes, I think my father was a little relieved, but I know he was soft-hearted when it came to the kids riding the buses. I remember a couple of the Model-T Ford buses he had in the late 20's. He also had two Reo buses, one normal-looking enclosed bus and the other an open-air thing with a long folding step along the right side. The enclosed Reo had two cylindrical things out in front, one on each side of the radiator. These were air-filled shock absorbers which had a regular tire valve on top, and in the spring when the buses were taken down off the blocks you would put an air hose on them and watch the front end of the bus rise a little as the shock absorbers were filled. They actually controlled the comfort of the ride, and of course helped to protect the general health of the bus. I used to think I was big-time when I was allowed to sit to the right of the driver in the open bus and work the folding step with the big iron lever—and most of the drivers were quite tolerant of the boss's funny little kid. Once in a while one would get a little impatient with me, especially if it became real busy; then I would take the hint and get lost.

The gas tank on the open-air Reo was right behind the windshield and in front of the steering wheel. This was also true in the case of all the Model A Ford cars and trucks. It certainly would not be allowed today. I do remember that a great many cars and small trucks

Newspaper photo of one of the buses in my father's Bathing Beach Bus Line, which ran from in front of the Atheneum to the Jetties and Cliffside beaches.

had their gas tanks under the front seats. (What a big hit that would make with today's safety-minded people!) The more common location for gas tanks was at the very rear of the vehicle, exposed just forward of the rear bumper, if the car was indeed equipped with the luxury of a rear bumper. Very dangerous by today's standards, these would be very hazardous for highway driving.

GREAT-GRANDPA MURPHEY & HIS HOUSE

During the Depression, my parents moved into the house at 19 Hussey Street—they had decided not to continue trying to spend each winter in Florida. At first I was distressed about this. I had several friends the same age in the Florida neighborhood and I missed them, and I also liked the warm weather. We lived just outside the city of St. Petersburg, and I remember that the menfolk would get together on occasion and burn off the tall grass in some of the empty land, mostly to protect us youngsters from snakes and other things. Once, my little friend Phillip Amic and I thought it would be a great idea to do it ourselves, especially since we had discovered a small box of matches in the lane behind our house. We picked an area of very tall grass and undergrowth and touched it off. It drew attention instantly, heading in the direction of several distant houses, and I think every able-bodied man in the neighborhood turned out in force to fight this conflagration started by two mischievous little kids. When he got back

19 Hussey Street, taken many years before my time, but showing the old Academy Hill School. The lady on the fronts steps is no doubt my grandmother whom I never knew.

to the house, my father immediately expressed his displeasure at what I had done, and it felt like he started another fire where I sat.

There were several reasons for my parents' decision not to return to Florida during the winters. One of them was economic; another was a matter of convenience for the rest of my father's family. My great-grandfather, Josiah F. Murphey, was living alone at 19 Hussey Street; he was quite elderly and needed someone else to be in the house. The move also solved a housing problem for us. It certainly worked out to the advantage of Grandpa Murphey, as well as my parents. He was very happy with the care he got from both my mother and father, particularly with my mother's cooking and housekeeping, and often expressed his satisfaction to her.

Grandpa was a very kindly and quiet old gentleman; I never heard him raise his voice. As one of the last three surviving Civil War veterans of Nantucket, he—along with Mr. James Barrett and Mr. James Wood—always addressed the Nantucket public school students from the pulpit of the Unitarian Church just prior to Memorial Day every year. Very seldom did Grandpa Murphey ever mention any of his experiences in the war, but I clearly remember my little bedroom being just above his and hearing the poor old man having horrendous nightmares, probably throwbacks to his war episodes. It surely scared the daylights out of me. I have been very fortunate in later years to come into possession of some of his war memoirs and a copy of the journal he kept throughout the war. I will never forget how nice he was, and how brokenhearted this eight-year-old kid was when he died at age 88. As I read of the different conflicts he endured, I saw that it was small wonder he suffered from nightmares in his later years. He had a deep scar on the right side of his face from a bullet he met in the street fighting of Fredericksburg on December 11, 1862. He was on the march to Gettysburg when he was stricken with typhoid and was sent to Alexandria to recuperate. When his enlistment was up, he was offered a captain's commission to re-enlist, but it wasn't his choice of life, so he declined. It is my understanding that he served in later years as Town Clerk, and also as Postmaster, in which order I don't know. In recent years a book [The Civil War: The Nantucket Experience, 1994] has been published by Robert Mooney and Richard Miller concerning Nantucket's participation in the Civil War, in which Grandpa Murphey is mentioned to quite some extent. The book even includes excerpts from the journal he kept during the war, which I think Mr. Miller found in a museum in Fredericksburg, Virginia. Very fascinating reading.

I recall that a lot of Grandpa Murphey's Civil War equipment was stored in the attic of 19 Hussey Street, and my grandmother took his musket, or rifle, whichever it was, and gave it to the local American Legion Post. I doubt if they could even identify which one it was now, if indeed they still have it. Rather a pity—it would have meant more to his survivors, I think. I do have a copy of his journal, thanks to Mr. Miller. I have read it cover to cover at least twice, and will again. His canteen wound up in my uncle's house in Florida, and I asked him to name his price for it, but he wasn't interested. He had it stored in his garden shed, of all places. I would have proudly displayed it in my office/den. I do believe he finally gave it to his daughter, who never knew the old gentleman. I just hope she knows its value, and carefully preserves it. There is little enough to remember those great men by.

When we moved into Grandpa Murphey's house, there were evidences of his frugalities, typical of that era. In the room above the kitchen were many bundles of neatly tied newspapers, which had been tunneled through by rodents. My father backed his old Reo truck up to the north window and with another man's help loaded them into the truck and delivered them to the town dump (then well out on the extension of Vestal Street, gradually working over in the direction of Hummock Pond Road). When my parents decided to buy the house from my grandparents in 1938 and do some renovations, one of the first things they had to do was to clean out hundreds of cans and bottles from under the southwest corner of the house. My father said he remembered Grandpa Murphey going out in the yard with a sack of those items, and lying on his stomach to throw them under the house. Hence, a few more trips to the dump. Since I was fifteen then, and the thinnest member of the family, I was delegated to crawl under there and throw them out so my father and brother could put them in trash barrels destined for the dump. Today many of them would probably be collector's items. It was an interesting old house, and in later years I opened a large fireplace in the dining room, which pleased my mother very much. There were some interesting artifacts found in there, too, including an old parasol which we have displayed in a shadow box, and some doll's clothing, quite likely my grandmother's, as she was born in that house. My wife very cleverly framed them under glass and they make an interesting display. I believe one can still read "J.F. Murphey" painted on one or two rafters in the attic. Being the sole owner of the house in more recent years, it was with mixed emotions that we finally sold it to some very nice people who could afford to do things with it that we never could, without going deeply in debt, and I had had enough of mortgages and related payments.

My father, his mother, her parents and grandparents were all born on Nantucket. My paternal grandfather, Byron E. Pease, was born in Edgartown and came to Nantucket as a very young man. He had a livery stable, which became a garage after cars were allowed on the island in 1918. It was located on the corner of South Water and Broad Streets opposite the Whaling Museum. Once, while he was on a visit to the Vineyard to see his family in Edgartown, the stable burned to the ground, and he lost several horses and much equipment. He immediately rebuilt it and retained it until my uncle Kenneth N. Pease took it over in 1945. Before my grandfather went into the livery business he and a Mr. Covil had operated a meat and grocery store on Main Street, on the ground floor of the Masonic

On the west side of 19 Hussey Street, in the rear, my father and great-grandfather Murphey, in the front row, myself and brother Donald, circa 1930.

building. Mr. Covil was also his partner in the livery business when it was first started.

MOTHER WAS A TEACHER

My mother was born in Mattapoisett and raised on a farm, which I always loved to visit when I was a youngster. My maternal grandfather was a very tall man, quite reserved, and very well respected in Mattapoisett. My two cousins from Weymouth, Bill and Jarvis Simpson, and I used to play on the living room rug and would get a little noisy and scrappy, but one word from Grandpa Ellis and all was quiet again. The farm is still very much there, but not farmed any more, and the area around it is now quite built up with some rather nice homes. Mother came to the island as a very young schoolteacher in 1916. Her summer job was "slinging hash," as she would have it, in the Nesbitt Inn on Broad Street. She stopped teaching, except for substituting, until some time during World War II, after we had left home, and continued teaching until she reached seventy years of age. In all, she taught three and four generations in some families. It's quite heartening to have her former pupils mention her. She preferred the real young ones, consequently she was very happy with her little first-graders. Due to her physical condition in her later years, it was not easy for her to get out from behind her desk, but she still maintained perfect control of a classroom of first-graders.

One summer my mother was obliged to go to Hyannis for quite a stretch of time, to take some teaching courses. My brother was farmed out to my grandparents' house in Federal Street, while I was more fortunate—I stayed with Mrs. Effie Coffin, later Effie Pond, on Milk Street. She was a wonderful person, and I enjoyed my stay very much. I must have been all of six or seven years old. My grandparents were apt to be more strict, which is why I felt so fortunate to stay with Effie Coffin. She and my mother were very close friends until Effie died in the late 1960's. I had due respect and regard for my grandparents—they were always very nice to us youngsters—and I just thought the world of Mrs. Coffin. Her first husband had died in the great flu epidemic of 1918. Her brother, George Lake, and his two daughters lived with Mrs. Coffin, Mr. Lake having lost his wife early in life. I had friends my age in that neighborhood anyway, Bill Gibbs,

Clifton Cady, and Teddy Jones, among others, so I was never lonesome.

Next door to my grandparents in Federal Street, number 12, lived an elderly lady, Mrs. Rickerson; my cousin's grandmother, Mrs. Simpson, was her housekeeper. My mother would visit once in a while, and I was obliged to tag along. Once I had a small American flag, which Mrs. Rickerson was admiring as she sat in her favorite rocker near the front door, the window to the left of it, as one faces the house. To amuse me, she asked me how many stars were in this flag, and I allowed as how I didn't know. So she suggested we count them; I diligently started to do this and probably got to four or maybe five when she said, "I counted 48," and it absolutely amazed me that she could count that many stars so quickly!

While my family lived in Vestal Street, an older boy, Stanley Roy, lived down the street from us, going west. I used to think this big guy was the salt of the earth, because for some weird reason he took a liking to me; he made a wooden toy airplane for me that I treasured for a long time. I still had it years later when we were living at 19 Hussey Street. I guess I was impressed because he was an older boy, and not many older boys tolerated the "little kids." Anyway, he impressed this little kid, and I always had a high regard for Stan.

For the first several years we lived at 19 Hussey Street, my mother was obliged to cook on an old black iron coal range, which also heated the water for our domestic hot water, in an upright copper tank that stood next to the stove. That stove produced some of the best food ever cooked, and it also was necessary for a major part of the heat in the house, the only other heat source being a small airtight wood stove in the living room. Since my father was in the cordwood business, the woodstove was a must, and coal was $14 a ton. As I recall cordwood sold for $18 per cord. The coal was delivered to the house, into a subcellar under the living room. This subcellar had a dirt floor, with a few well-placed stepping stones, because often there would be water on the floor following a heavy wet spell. It was one of my jobs to keep the coal range supplied with coal. My father insisted on taking out the ashes himself, thereby minimizing the dust. That didn't displease me at all. In one corner of this subcellar was an old brick cistern, which had a very sad memory for me, as one of my cats died in it. In later years my interest in cats was, and still is, nil. In the woodshed adjoining the northwest corner of the house was a small gas range that we cooked on in the summer, when the coal range could be shut down. I popped corn on that gas stove a great many times, and to this day popcorn is one of my favorite foods. There was also a real "icebox" in that shed, and I can remember how thankful I was that no pan under it ever had to be emptied, since it drained into a hole my father had arranged in the cement floor when he poured it. I came home one day and heard a small commotion in that area, and went into the kitchen to see what was going on. I encountered my father trying to coax a piece of ice into the proper compartment, but the ice was just a shade too big, and he was trying to convince it to go in by kicking it...or it might be better to say he was trying to push it in with his foot. At any rate, he wasn't being very gentle about it, nor very successful, much to my amusement, but I knew better than to let him see me laughing, so I beat a hasty retreat. I recall my mother complaining soon after about things being tipped over in the icebox, at which time I tried to display total ignorance of the entire episode.

All three bedrooms upstairs at 19 Hussey Street were very cold in the winter months, therefore turning in at night and turning out in the morning were always done with well-timed brevity. I once had a bottle of ink freeze in my bedroom. It is very true, we indeed do not get the cold winters we used to have. At my present age I don't regret that too much, but I am sorry for the kids, that they don't get to enjoy the winter skating we did. However, it is a little reassuring that the long grass is cut each fall at the old Mill Pond on New Lane, and provisions made for flooding it, should we get some proper freezing weather. We youngsters of the 1930's passed hundreds of happy hours skating there.

SUMMER ENTERTAINMENTS

In those years there was always a county fair in the month of August. The fairground was located on the spot where the Nantucket Electric Company now has its office and workshop. One of the big attractions of the fair was the trotting race. I can't remember all the sulky owners, but Barclay Vincent, Charles Thurston, and I think Irvin Wyer had sulkies. Some of the many dairy farmers would be exhibiting their cows, chickens, pigs, and produce. There were several dairy farms on the island then, the largest being that of John H. Bartlett, Sr., with over a hundred cows; Edouard O. Gardner and Harry A. Larrabee (both on Hummock Pond Road); John Roberts on Somerset Road; Richard Brooks in North Liberty Street; Mr. Holmes of Nobadeer Farm, now the airport; and also Ezra Lewis, Mr. Dawson, Matthew Jaeckle, and Mr. Clisby in Milk Street, all on a smaller scale than Bartlett's.

In the thirties, I remember one summer, I was then a grade-schooler, a Mr. Edward McHugh, "The Gospel Singer of the Air," was scheduled to come to the island. He was to come to the Congregational ("North") Church, and somehow I became one of the ticket-sellers, going door to door. Mr. McHugh had a remarkable voice, and was well known nationally, so it was no trouble to sell tickets, and I sold better than two hundred. I clearly remember attending his performance. How I wish we could hear that type of singing today. His voice easily filled that big church without the benefit of electronic amplification. I seem to recall that he had a daily radio program, too. He would start his program by singing a hymn type of theme song, "If I Have Injured Any Soul Today," in his very rich, resonant voice.

Another very pleasant scene on summer evenings was Herbert Brownell playing his accordion on Main Street. Herbie was blind but quite talented, and friendly with everybody. In later years a Mr. William "Billy" Fitzgerald would lead people in singing along with Herbie, and the crowd would become rather large, spilling out into Main Street. The vehicular traffic of those years was nothing like today's, so it presented very little, if any, problem. Herbie was a native, but I think Mr. Fitzgerald came from the Boston area. He was a very pleasant and attractive man, who later became badly afflicted with arthritis and had to walk with two canes, though he was not an old man by any means.

I also remember three young men who would come to the island and perform downtown in the evening. Each played an accordion, and very well. They would play on the steps of the Pacific National Bank, one of them walking around some, passing the hat, or another receptacle. Fortunately for Herb Brownell they never stayed on the island very long.

Then there was an older lady, I think her name was Miss Helen

McLeary, and she used to come down to Main Street in the evening and accompany Herbie Brownell, playing her "spoons." She was always dressed in typical late Victorian style, which included a wide-brimmed hat with pom-poms hanging all around the brim. She never smiled, which added to the amusement. She would also ride my father's buses to the beach, but always stood out on the sidewalk complaining that the bus didn't leave as soon as she was ready. This amused my father or any driver on duty, as well as all the passengers waiting patiently in the buses. Maybe she knew what she was doing. I recall her once announcing to all present that she was going to start her own bus line!

Also, in the winter months there would be performers at the North Church Vestry. They came from some kind of a syndicated entertainment service known as the Collins Festivals. One was a deep-sea diver, Mr. Zimmerman, who gave a lecture and showed a lot of his diving equipment and artifacts; he had some wonderful tales to tell us youngsters. There were musicians and choral groups, also. When none of these were available there might be a Saturday-night or Saturday-afternoon movie at either the North Church or the Methodist Church, and they even had sound, believe it or not. In the winter months there would be movies on Wednesdays and Saturdays at the Dreamland Theater, beginning at 7:30 p.m. and usually running no later than 9:15 or 9:30. Some were even in Technicolor, which was not common then. In the summer months there were movies every night, one at 7:30 and the late show usually starting about 9:30. There were movies at the 'Sconset Casino, but I never happened to

Main Street at the corner of Union Street, partially showing the Masonic building on the very left, the home of Nantucket Masonry, Union Lodge F & AM, which has had a big effect on my life.

— *Photo courtesy of the Nantucket Historical Association*

make it to any. It was a big thrill whenever we got off-island and visited a "big city," like New Bedford, and were able to go to a bona fide theater and see a double feature, newsreels, the whole shebang, and probably all for a dime.

There was a stretch of time when the "summer people" thought it would be real quaintsy to have a town crier, as in days of old. And we indeed had one—I can't remember how long it took for the novelty to wear off, but it didn't last long. We had only the Inquirer and Mirror for a weekly paper; it came out every Friday and sold for ten cents. It never had any competition until after World War II, when the Town Crier came into being, ran for several years, and then sold out to the Inquirer and Mirror. I think the Boston daily papers sold for something like three cents back in the thirties, and the Sunday edition cost ten cents. The daily papers had a weather forecast that was very brief, and usually started "for Boston and vicinity..." Forecasts were also available on broadcast radio; these were equally accurate, and usually started out with the announcer saying "from Eastport to Block Island," or "from Eastport to Sandy Hook," which covered quite a forecast area. My father simply watched the barometer and the wind directions more than anything else. My great-grandfather had a unique old barometer, which I now have, and which he insisted had to be outdoors. It hung out on the north side of the house, near the back door. According to the face of it, it was made by "Pike, 518 Broadway, New York." It is not very sensitive any more, or accurate, but it's a memory, nevertheless.

THE GREAT DEPRESSION

One big advantage we had here on Nantucket during the miserable years of the Depression was the fact that our parents could avail themselves of a lot of food provided by nature. We ate bluefish, eels, clams, quahogs, scallops, rabbits, pheasants, ducks, geese, and venison, all of which could be prepared in several different ways. Fish could be bought for very little right from a fishing boat at the dock; today, the "authorities" won't allow that, the authorities in this case being the state. I believe this has to do with retailing, more than likely the fish markets complaining about the practice of dockside retailing. One winter in particular we seemed to have plenty of meat, and I was old enough then to realize that my parents didn't have money to spare for expensive meat. Once in a while my father would go upstairs to the room above the kitchen, and I could hear him removing a metal cover from a large round tin. It was cold in that room, and that was where he was storing the very fresh venison. I don't ever recall him shooting a deer "in season." It was also very fortunate for us that my mother was such a superb cook. Fortunately for me, I liked to eat and she liked to cook. I am still trying to duplicate the chowders she would make. Not enough credit can be given her for the many wonderful things she did, not only in our own home, by any means. In our generous-sized yard were some fruit trees that my great-grandfather had planted when he was a young man; they bore pears, plums, and quinces, all of which my mother would preserve for winter use. In the summer my father would buy a large amount of fresh eggs and preserve them in a five-gallon earthenware crock in the small sub-cellar of the house in a solution known as "water glass." Dad would buy a bushel of peaches which my mother would preserve, along with beach plum and grape jellies. The carrots and beets would stay in the ground all winter, and often I was sent out to chop some out of the frozen ground for dinner. The frost didn't seem to bother them much.

I was, and still am, impressed with the fact that my father never drew a dime's worth of any kind of relief in those years and he always managed to produce something, somehow—even to seining Long Pond for herring in the spring, and selling herring roe and smoked herring. He built our garage in Crown Court and mounted a Model-T Ford engine in its southeast corner, with an exhaust pipe going out under the foundation. This powered a big saw table where he cut cordwood that he had shipped in from the mainland. I still have one of the big saw blades, about twenty inches in diameter, and I can still hear that thing whirring as the engine picked up speed. It would slide through a thick oak log like the proverbial hot knife through soft butter. On more than one weekend I would be elected, by a unanimous vote of one, to help him haul the uncut logs up from the steamboat dock and stack them in the garage, two rows deep and at least six feet high. These things he did, a man with a badly damaged heart. Whether it hastened his demise or kept him going that long is anybody's guess, but he only made it to age 47.

A particularly big treat for me in those years was being allowed to spend a week or two with one of my mother's aunts in New Bedford, and even take my bike with me. The round-trip fare on the steamers for a youngster then was $4.10, including the bike. From her house in Park Street I could ride in any direction, such as South Dartmouth where I could go aboard the whaleship Charles W. Morgan. Or I would ride across the Fairhaven bridge to visit other relatives in Mattapoissett, or "up country" to Uncle Henry Howard's farm. Another favorite haunt was Acushnet Park, the amusement park in the south end of New Bedford, near Fort Rodman. What a horrible thought, a youngster even thinking of doing that in this day and age. The speeds and volume of traffic make it virtually impossible.

Another exciting event in my boyhood life occurred on my brother's birthday in August; my father took us both out to the airport, where he hired the popular local pilot, Ray Morrison, to take us up for our very first plane ride. It was an old Stinson, which bumped along the bare sod field and finally became airborne. During the big harbor "freeze-up" one winter, we Nantucket kids probably saw more aircraft in one short week than any kid in the country. It seemed as if they were coming and going all day long, every day. The news media, being no more accurate then than it is now, had stories of the Nantucket people being near starvation due to the freeze-up, yet all the stores were well stocked with fresh fruit, vegetables, meat, and so on. I was once scheduled, by my grandfather, to fly home from New Bedford aboard a Stinson tri-motored plane of Mayflower Airlines, created, owned and operated by Parker Gray, Sr., but somehow the schedule was different than my source of information and I missed it, very much to my chagrin.

With the advent of World War II, the U.S. Navy took over the airport, expanded and paved it, and since those years it has become the second busiest airport in Massachusetts and the second busiest in New England in the summer months. So much for progress. Before the war, the airport had consisted of a large area of mowed grass, one small corrugated sheet-metal hangar big enough to accommodate one small plane, and an old bus body for an office. The navigational instrumentation was one windsock.

We were certainly remotely located, and there seemed to be

little for kids to do in those years. However, we always seemed to be able to occupy ourselves with some type of diversion, even without a Boys Club or an Olympic-sized swimming pool (or any swimming pool, for that matter). As I mentioned earlier, we did have a Boy Scout troop, and Rev. Fred Bennett introduced basketball to the island in the 1930's. Every once in a great while there would indeed be a case of juvenile delinquency, never anything real serious, and there certainly were no drugs in our school. In those years we didn't even know what "drugs" were, other than pharmacy prescriptions.

BOY SCOUTS, SCHOOLDAYS

In 1935 I became a Boy Scout. The town troop then was Troop 92, and the one in 'Sconset was Troop 95. There was no competition between the two that I remember— Troop 95 was quite some smaller than Troop 92, naturally, and met in the 'Sconset schoolhouse. Troop 92 met in Legion Hall, and among other activities we had an occasional camping trip when conditions permitted. Our leaders had somehow come into possession of some World War I army tents and folding cots, which afforded some pretty good camping luxuries. For leaders we had Leo Ashe, Ralph Smith (both schoolteachers), Albert Fee, Roy Studley, Norman Giffin, Charlie Handy (in 'Sconset) and my father, among others whose names I can't recall at the moment. Very few boys from Nantucket attended things like the National Jamboree, due mostly to finances and location. Scouting activities were pretty nice things to have then, there being no boys' club or television, among many other things that are available today. In the late 1950's I was pressured into becoming the Scoutmaster of Troop 97. I agreed to take it "for a year." Six years later I indeed had to relinquish the job, because my commitments to my mother and her elderly aunt's needs were increasing and required much more of my time. However, it was one of the very pleasant experiences of my life.

On Hussey Street we lived only a few yards from the school, which precluded any excuse for me being late for classes. And to make bad matters worse, for several years my father was the "attendance officer", making it just about impossible for his pride and joy to play truant. The only time I ever got away with anything like that was when I was in high school. I managed, quite successfully, to be among the missing for an afternoon session because I had his car, and was supposed to be doing something else instead of swimming in the surf.

One of my very early recollections of school on Nantucket took place in the new Academy Hill building, in the first grade. Our teacher had cause to step out of the room briefly, and of course pandemonium reigned while she was out. Forever after, I marveled at the accomplishment of Morey Lewis. Somehow he had softened a crayon sufficiently so that when he threw it up to the ceiling it stuck. It stayed there for several years. He really left his mark.

It wasn't always easy for the town officials to procure good professional people, but I think they did pretty well at getting teachers to come to the island. They didn't all want to stay, but fortunately for us some very good ones did stay. Among my favorites was Mrs. Howard Chase, our fifth-grade teacher; she was a most understanding and compassionate teacher. Mrs. Swayze always impressed us too; she had a unique way of letting all hands know she wasn't satisfied with our conduct—a rather profound expression of the word "WELL!" It worked every time. I remember one incident in her classroom: I think she was trying to fill time until the bell, and still hold our attention. Everybody was to write the name of a flower that began with the letter C. Yours truly, being a little bored with this game, wrote down the word "cauliflower," which amused the entire class, but not Mrs. Swayze. I can't remember my penalty for that, but it was fun, anyway.

We didn't have many men teachers. Mr. Richard Porter was one who impressed me. Having been to Virginia Military Academy, he had a certain military bearing about himself. He never raised his voice, and by nature seemed to command a degree of respect. He was a very good math teacher—he could even make me understand it. During World War II, Mr. Porter became superintendent of schools. Mr. Ralph Smith was also a good teacher, but one of his subjects was Ancient History, which bored me to death at the time; however, with quite some effort I managed to pass.

Without exception, the teacher who made the deepest impression on me was Mr. Alvin E. Paddack. Now there was a teacher with no "formal" education, but with a very scientific mind. He was our Coffin School teacher, and taught us many skills besides woodworking, such as blueprinting, isometric drawing, blueprint reading, and pattern-making on wood-turning lathes. In instructing us on the use of power tools and sharp instruments, he had a rather unique bit of caution for us: "Now please, boys, don't get any blood on the tools!" He even had us do a detailed drawing and blueprint of the entire Coffin School building itself. As well, he was personally responsible for helping several boys through advanced education after they left high school. Whether he knew it or not, he also taught us a lot about respect and conduct. Mr. Paddack was yet another teacher who never raised his voice. He never had need to, because by his nature he commanded our attention and respect, and we were never bored.

The first athletic coach our school system ever had was Harry Cleverly. Although I was not a gung-ho athlete, I liked Mr. Cleverly, as did just about everybody else. He was somewhat short of stature, but a real live wire. One day one of the older boys was obliged to stay after school for some reason, and as Mr. Cleverly was talking to him, the boy gave a flip answer, which proved to be a big mistake on his part. The next thing he knew he was sitting on the floor. Just let a teacher even think about doing that today, and he would wind up in court and out of a job! More's the pity.

MR. PADDACK'S GARDEN

One of my favorite memories concerning Mr. Paddack was the large vegetable garden he used to have in Lily Street, on the north side of Mr. Giffin's carpenter shop. I believe Mr. Giffin owned the land and gave Mr. Paddack the use of it. Mr. Paddack always lived in a rented room, and as far as I know never did any cooking for himself, taking all his meals in restaurants. He gave away everything he grew, and I can see him now, toiling by the hour in his garden. It was not unusual to see him on weekends walking in remote areas of the island, always by himself. As long as his health allowed, he remained active in the Coffin School. He was a very quiet and highly respected man. In his last years he rented a room from Mrs. Annette Stackpole in Bloom Street, and often I would see him walking home after leaving a local restaurant, and would offer him a ride. He almost always declined, but a few times he accepted, and it was obvious he wasn't feeling very well. I believe Mrs. Stackpole was very nice to him and looked after

22

him for quite some, other than just renting a room to him. I'm sure there are many of us who will never forget Mr. Paddock. (Many of us won't forget Mrs. Stackpole, as well.)

If you lived on the north side of town you went to the Academy Hill School on Westminster Street, in which case you spent the years from grades one through twelve in the same building, unless you took some courses in the Coffin School. Those living on the south side of town were obliged to attend the Cyrus Peirce School until they reached the seventh grade, when they were transferred to Academy Hill. One educator told me that in the 1950's the Cyrus Peirce school was way ahead of its time, being a more modern type of school building. If one lived in 'Sconset, he or she attended the one-room schoolhouse until sixth or seventh grade age. Others were bussed in from Madaket, Hummock Pond, Surfside, Wauwinet, and Polpis. (Nowadays the school kids seem to be bussed in from "around the corner.") Academy Hill was still the base of operations, though. I can't say that we were ever hard put for something to do, considering the different activities within the various churches and the school system. There was a certain amount of drinking in later school years, but I don't ever remember anyone getting into trouble over it. I could never acquire a taste or desire for any of it until long after my school years, thankfully.

The Academy Hill School was indeed quite a building, and it is still standing, not as a school, but as an apartment building for seniors. My father used to complain that it had cost $250,000 to build the school in 1929, and as much more to keep it there the next few years.

The old Academy Hill School, the educational locale, this and the Coffin School.

I clearly remember the northeast wind driving the rain through the brick walls, and seeing the water run in rivulets along the corridors. The contractor was then required to waterproof the outside. The heating system was interesting, too. There were two huge steam boilers in the basement and cast-iron radiators in each classroom which hissed, clanked, and wheezed whenever heat was required. The pipes leading to the radiators were encased in asbestos covers with small steel straps holding them in place. One could give them a slight nudge and see the asbestos escape in white, powdery puffs. Where were the lifesaving "environmentalists" then? They could have had a field day with that situation. Amazingly, we all survived the evils of asbestos.

We were always told that the Academy Hill building was put there through petty local politics, and that it was supposed to have been located in the Mackay property near the Mill Pond, rather than on the site of the old wooden Academy Hill School. I can barely remember that old wooden building, walking by it with my mother on our way to Sunday School at the Congregational Church. Years after it was removed and the new building erected, we could always see rusty nails in the school playground. Two old houses stood very close to the southeast corner of the building, making the ground-floor classroom in that corner very dark, even on sunny days. Mrs. Howard Chase had her fifth grade in that room. Fortunately she was an excellent teacher, and that made up for a lot of the dark gloom of the room.

I will never forget Donald Dunbar in Mrs. Chase's fifth grade. She had called on Donald to stand and read from a certain storybook, and when he came to the word "bazaar," he paused, studied it for a moment, and came out with "brassiere," at which point Mrs. Chase went into gales of laughter...and some of us understood why. That was far better than my "cauliflower" episode with Mrs. Swayze. In those years a teacher was not required to "spare the rod," and on rare occasions physical punishment was administered. I was the recipient of it on more than one occasion, and you can believe I kept my mouth shut about it at home.

24

HIGH JINKS

Once, Donald Dunbar and I were walking along Federal Street, on the sidewalk by the Atheneum Library, and there were small puddles on the bricks which we were making good use of by stamping our feet in them trying to soak each other. We succeeded a little too well, spattering two ladies who were wearing the traditional silk stockings. They expressed their displeasure and ordered us to go right home. The nearest home being Donald's, the old Sanford House that the present town building replaced, we started in that direction with the two ladies carefully following us. Donald was pretty sharp, and under his breath he suggested to me that we walk right past his house, and take a mixed course. After turning several corners, we lost the offended ladies, and went on to some other mischief. We were probably all of eight or ten years old then.

During the presidential campaign of 1936, one of my compatriots and I hit upon a clever idea. A bandstand had been set up on Main Street just opposite the end of Federal Street, and a lively amount of political rhetoric, Democrat style, was flowing forth, complete with a band playing. We hotfooted it over to Miss Stevens' store in Center Street because we knew she had a bountiful supply of Republican leaflets, which she was glad to give to us, and we circulated them among the crowd of onlookers and listeners of the Democrat show. It didn't seem to have any affect on the national election, but we were optimistic about it, anyway.

More than once I was admonished by others for not being a "gung-ho" athlete. I tried playing basketball, but I was required to wear the wire-cage-like thing to protect my glasses, and I certainly couldn't see well enough to play without them. That, of course, wiped out any prospect of playing football. The high school athletic program then included only football and basketball. I think I could have done well in track, but it wasn't in the program then. I used to run some distances, and did fairly well at it. I certainly got enough exercise on my bike, and I swam a lot in warm weather, and skated a lot in cold weather. The large amount of rowing I did certainly didn't hurt me any, either. Having always been quite active physically, gaining weight has never been a problem for me.

On the subject of swimming, in my high school years Roger Young lived next door to my family in Hussey Street, on the east side of Westminster Street, and for one summer at least, when we got through work in the late afternoon, the two of us would get into our bathing trunks, hop into one of my father's cars, and drive out to the surf at the end of Hummock Pond Road for a quick swim. Then we'd go to Allen's Diner for our evening meal. On one such occasion the surf was quite lively. Roger dove in and got out beyond the breakers before I could get there. Throwing caution to the winds I dove in too, but didn't make out as well as Roger, for I promptly got "boiled" in the breakers—it felt as if my back was breaking. I got out OK, but had some interesting raw places on my face as well as a large scrape on my chest that I was able to conceal. And of course Bill Allen, at the diner, had to ask, "What did the other guy look like?" I continued to swim in the surf, but after that incident I was a little more circumspect about it.

GOING FISHING, GETTING HOME ON TIME

Mr. Whittemore Gardner's little store at the monument on Main Street was one of the leading attractions of our neighborhood. It was a typical country grocery—a barrel of molasses, one of sugar, one of flour, crackers also in bulk, and a little box for us little kids to hop up on to choose what penny candy we wanted. Often my mother sent me to the store with maybe fifteen cents and a gallon jug to be filled with molasses. This small building was recently condemned and removed, and that was quite a controversial subject on the island. Another attraction nearby was Mr. Worth's ice cream store, across Main Street and a little east. He made all his ice cream right on the premises, and needless to say, it was exceptional.

At some point, I bought a second bike for fifty cents. It needed a few things that I was able to buy or find. I repainted it and had another pretty good bike. I was so proud of my accomplishment I refused several offers to buy it. My first bike had been a purchase from the Montgomery Ward Company for $15. It had "balloon" tires, which were the trend then, and chrome fenders that never rusted. This model was always bright and easy to shine.

I liked to fish when I was a grade-schooler. It was common practice for two or three of us to pack a lunch and hike or bike to

Wannacomet Pond and catch white perch and bluegills. In Hummock Pond we would get yellow perch, and in Long Pond it was white perch and pickerel. And I never had trouble finding someone to go with me in the skiff to fish in the harbor for scup. One day Wayman Coffin went with me and we were fishing off the starboard side of the skiff getting nothing. He asked me which side of the skiff we had fished from the previous day, and I said "this side," and he promptly pulled his line in, saying the reason we were getting no fish was that we had caught all the ones on that side. He threw his line over the other side and, of course, started catching fish. I don't think I caught any—I was too busy laughing at him. He was always good for a laugh, and still is. As I mentioned earlier, it was not unusual for us to net a couple bucks by selling the scup to the yacht people anchored nearby. Once the shellfish warden got very upset with Tom Giffin and me for digging soft-shell clams in the murky mud of Easy Street, a polluted area even then. When we explained we were using them only for scup bait, his blood pressure went back to normal.

Another money-making enterprise was to row over to Coatue and pick a bushel box (swiped from the grocery store) full of saltmarsh rosemary, tie it into small bouquets, and sell them on Main Street for a dime a bunch. Considering it was during the mid-1930's, and considering the operating expense, we were making big money.

An older gentleman by the name of Russell Pemberton boarded with my parents. He was a quiet, gentle sort and I liked him very

Captain Zeb Tilton's schooner, Alice T. Wentworth, on which I sailed one day as a very young kid. Here she is being pushed into the harbor by her yawl boat.

— *Photo courtesy of the Nantucket Historical Association*

27

much. He was very good to me, teaching me things about fishing and setting me up with rod and reel. In the summer he ran a small cabin cruiser that took out parties. Once he was taking the boat to Madaket and allowed me to come along. It turned out to be a very blustery day, and we had a headwind all the way to Madaket. He let me take the wheel, and deliberately went below and stayed there, while this twelve-year-old had the time of his life. I was already hopelessly "hooked" on boats and the water, and this little trip just cemented it more. Mr. Pemberton had a Model A Ford business coupe, with normal-sized tires on it. He would soften the tires and drive it all the way to the end of Smith Point to fish, and never get stuck. Of course that was years before four-wheel drives, when the sand didn't get cut up into so much loose base. Russell Pemberton worked as a carpenter in the winter months. He moved away from the island during the war, and it was a sad day for me when I heard on the radio news that he had died suddenly, digging clams in Mattapoisett.

I didn't have the luxury of a watch in those days, but I didn't care much about what time it was anyway. I was supposed to be home sometime between five and six p.m. If I was on the beach at Coatue in the afternoon, the steamer Martha's Vineyard would let out a long blast on her steam whistle at 4:45, warning all the tourists it was about to leave at 5:00 p.m. That was my signal to pick up and row for Easy Street, and I was usually in the Easy Street basin when the boat gave one more short toot fifteen minutes later, and left.

Easy Street on a typical summer day, with an artist on the scene. The steamer Martha's Vineyard is at the end of the wharf, as is the Skipper Restaurant with the old coal schooner Allen Gurney, slowly decaying.

— *Photo courtesy of the Nantucket Historical Association*

ISLAND WINTERS

My first recollection of snow was on Thanksgiving Day in 1928 or '29. Even though I had been born on the island, my family's winters in Florida prevented me from seeing any snow that I could remember until then. I thought it was great fun to stamp my feet in the slushy stuff on the pavement and watch it fly in all directions, until I realized my feet were painfully cold as a result. Nantucket's winters then were more severe than now, so my acquaintance with snow soon became more intimate. It was just before the drainage system of the Lily Pond was perfected that I learned to skate there, using an old pair of skates that clamped onto my shoes, producing blisters in odd locations on my feet. My love for skating persisted, and eventually I graduated to shoe skates, which I still had and used shortly after the war, and any time we had proper ice I would hike to Maxcy's Pond, among other ponds, to skate, day or night. We used to have some great bonfires in the middle of Maxcy's Pond. It was also there that I cracked a bone in my elbow as a result of roughhousing on the ice, and I had to wear my arm in a cast for six weeks.

Then there was the big "freeze-up" many of us can remember in the mid-1930's, and we skated all over Nantucket Harbor, clear to Wauwinet. There were iceboats galore, including one contrived by Harry Gordon powered by a motorcycle engine and a salvaged airplane propeller. How well I remember Andrew Swain and how he would build up speed and jump clear over a catboat on its mooring...until one day he did too well at it and the ice let go where he landed, so he received a chilly dunking. He was one of the most athletic boys of our era, and a great runner. Years later, skating on Coventry Lake in Connecticut in 1942, I learned to use a hand-held sail, which brought some interesting results. One either learns to tack or have one long headwind trip back. A "crash" course in skate sailing, you could say.

Another big attraction in the winter was being present when the steamers were either trying to get into or out of the icebound harbor. This would attract small crowds just for the sake of watching. My mother once had to resort to flying to East Fairhaven, there having been a death in her family in Mattapoisett, because no boats were able to come to or leave the island.

Once in the 1930's, we had a major sleet storm which, when it finally stopped, left a very hard crust everywhere. John Toner, one of my classmates, and I would put our skates on just outside the school door and skate wherever we wanted to go—usually over the fields to the Mill Pond on New Lane, and then off in a westerly direction from there. I even hitched a ride behind a horse-drawn sleigh in Centre Street, a bit safer than grabbing hold of a truck's tailgate while on a bike. I did that too, on rare occasions.

Even though automobiles were allowed on the island in 1918, there were still quite a few horse-drawn vehicles when we were kids. Notable among them were all the ice wagons of John R. Killen Co., located on Straight Wharf. The one that served our neighborhood was driven by a genial old man named Caesar Lopes (at least he seemed old to a little kid), and this seven-year-old would stand at the curb in front of Mr. Crocker's house next door to us in Hussey Street, with several apples, pears, quinces, or whatever else I could swipe for the horse. My reward for this was being allowed to drive the horse for the next two or three stops. John K. Ayers also operated his plumbing business from a horse-drawn wagon, even though he drove around in a new Buick sedan. I can see that portly gentleman now, very properly dressed in a brown business suit and straw hat, driving his wagon loaded with plumbing tools and pipes. Because he was a business partner of my grandfather's in the garage and taxi operation, I was allowed to hitch a ride with him and drive his horse. I recall once seeing a horse, complete with saddle but missing a rider, going "full tilt" through Milk Street headed for town. I also recall that there were several surreys that were always lined up at the steamboat landing in the summer season to pick up passengers. They would even display a "Taxi" sign. Many of us can remember the taxis of Mr. Wood, Mr. Backus, Mr. Coffin, and Mr. Thurston, among others.

Our favorite sledding spots when conditions permitted were Mill Hill down to Pleasant Street, Dead Horse Valley, still a popular spot, Orange Street onto Main when the police would cordon it off for us as they still do occasionally, Step Lane, and the steep bank at the Sea Cliff Inn. There was a choice of routes at the Sea Cliff Inn, either down the path that led to Beach Road or right down the embankment, which had a broad bump at the bottom that would allow one to become airborne for a few feet. A favorite trick on the Orange Street run was for the "big guys" to run alongside as you started down the hill and jump on top of the smaller guys and get a free ride. One such big guy was running alongside me one night with that intent, and I reached out with one arm and tripped him. The last I saw of him he was tumbling among the slush and ice. I decided that one run was about enough for that night and went elsewhere with my sled, in case he remembered me.

One incident that never left my mind occurred when the very personable Gilbert Wyer was driving the school bus for John Terry. It was quite cold, with plenty of snow on the ground. "Gibby" was returning from his 'Sconset run, going through Union Street, when out of the corner of his eye he saw a youngster sliding down Flora Street into Union Street, just at the last fatal moment. There was no stopping, but the youngster had presence of mind enough to roll off his sled and let it go under the bus. Of course at that point Gibby couldn't see the youngster any more, since it had all happened in scant seconds. I think the whole incident must have proven that Gibby had a very strong heart.

Gibby was a person who was always fond of kids and nice to them. On Halloween night he would always be downtown handing out tickets to the kids to go to Toner's Drugstore and get an ice cream cone. His strategy must have been to keep the little brats out of trouble for at least a little while, but we certainly respected him for it.

MISCHIEF & DERRING-DO

Speaking of flying through the air, there used to be a nice shortcut through the Lily Pond from North Liberty Street to Lily Street. We would ride our bikes down Mr. Lincoln Lewis' driveway in Lily Street, take a quick right turn through an opening in the fence, and pedal as hard as we could along the path until we came to a mound that crossed the path which would allow us to become airborne. I once covered six feet of ground in the air. I think we covered the ground with ourselves a few times, too. This same path also provided a shortcut for a lot of kids going to and coming from school, kids from the "Egypt" area. Another stunt of derring-do was to ride down the steps in front of the North Church onto Centre Street, and the same

31

thing in Stone Alley, going out onto Union Street. We didn't do these things habitually, as the wear and tear on the bikes would be too much, and we were responsible for our own repairs and costs.

There was a Mr. Dawson who had a milk route through our neighborhood, with a typical old-style milk wagon, like the one in the Pepperidge Farm commercials of several years ago. Well, Mr. Dawson never seemed to talk kindly to his horse, so we kids would hide behind a nearby fence or hedge and wait for Mr. Dawson to get just at the door of the house with his bottles of milk; then we would imitate his voice and encourage the horse to take off without Mr. Dawson. This produced some interesting motion on the part of that gentleman; it also improved our ability to disappear in a hurry.

Being adventurous as well as mischievous, Clifton Cady and I were once down by the Dreamland Theater, on the north side of the building, and we encountered Lawrence Cahoon, who somehow had come into possession of a package of cigarettes. Cliff was very anxious to get one from him, but Lawrence allowed as how we were much too young. However, Cliff persisted, telling Lawrence, who must have been all of twelve or thirteen, that he was eight years old, and therefore not so young. Fortunately for us, Lawrence was persistent and refused. Even though I was only eight myself, I wasn't very chagrined at Cliff's failure. As young as I was, I knew smoking would only make us sick. I must have had a previous experience, I don't recall.

At about the same era I was once rummaging around in back of the theater, for no good reason, and the boy I was with found a dollar bill—not a common item in the Depression years. What makes me remember this more vividly was that his mother doubted if he had indeed found it. I felt so badly for him, that his mother would doubt his veracity, even when I tried to back him up. He was a nice kid, and we got along well together.

We had our mean streaks at that age, and were fairly inventive at exhibiting them. One handy gadget we made use of was a medium-sized spike, with some heavy cord tied to it head, knotted all along its three-foot length. We would slip the spike up under a shingle on the side of a house, usually right next to the window where somebody would be sitting quite peacefully. By pulling back on the string and

32

running the knots between the thumb and forefinger, we could produce a noise that sounded as if every shingle was coming off the side of the house at once. It didn't do any damage, except to the nerves of the recipient, and it also improved our ability to vanish into the night.

Yet another handy little device was a tin can with one end out of it (there was never a shortage of these) with a hole punched in the center of the remaining end, a piece of stout twine, well coated with beeswax, through the hole. Drawing that twine between the thumb and forefinger would produce some interesting shrieking noises. Oh well, at least it was better than smashing mailboxes, which I never heard of any of our peers doing.

Evaporated-milk cans were also used in a novel way. If you put one on the ground and stamped your feet on it, it would tend to clinch over the edges of your shoe soles and stay there until removed by hand. Several of us would equip ourselves so, and in running along the pavement we liked to think we were a herd of wild horses. Some of the neighbors got the same impression and expressed their disapproval.

The aforementioned instruments of annoyance were handy on Halloween nights, too, as were bean-blowers. One Halloween evening, I was with a compatriot and we were walking along Centre Street, between Hussey and India Streets. Along came a car driven by one of the local constabulary, and this little brat had nothing better to do than blow some beans at the rear of said vehicle, which instantly stopped and started to back up to apprehend the two culprits. Of course we weren't going to be "run in" by the local lawmen, so we hotfooted it into Hussey Street, clambered over Emma Cook's fence, darted across the yard to Quince Street, made a beeline up Quince Street, through the south playground of Academy Hill School, into Lily Street, onto the porch of a house bordering on the Lily Pond, and along the porch to some steps that went down into the back lawn of the house. These steps and the deck above them were very damp, and slicker than grease, therefore causing this lawbreaker, yours truly, to make it down the steps without touching any of them with my feet. We then disappeared into the jungle of the Lily Pond, making good our escape from the law.

... & OTHER ADVENTURES

Once, Clifton Cady and I were on that section of Vestal Street extension which borders on the south edge of the Quaker Cemetery, but just inside the fence well along that border, Teddy Jones's father, who was a landscape gardener, had a greenhouse, and he got rightfully nervous about having two young brats, anywhere near it. We had probably been throwing stones or whatever, and Mr. Jones didn't waste any time in suggesting that we get out of the area, for very obvious reasons, and he was rather persuasive about it. There was no doubt in what he meant, and he was very convincing. We decided we didn't like his old greenhouse, anyway. The town dump was farther west on Vestal Street, and there were no houses in that area then—you'd have thought we'd head for that, but I guess the dump didn't interest us very much—I don't recall ever spending much time there.

Our neighborhood had its share of youngsters in it: the Lamb family, Roger Young, David Conway, Tom Giffin, George Thatchell, Gilbert Reed, the two Anderson brothers, Bill Ratcliffe and his brother Jimmy, and others whose names I don't recall; and because Academy Hill School was in the neighborhood, its open playgrounds would attract kids from other parts of the town. There would be members of the Colby family, Doug Blanchard, Eddy Quigley, and others from the "Egypt" area. (This was what the areas of town near the intersection of North Liberty and West Chester Streets. Another prolific neighborhood. I never did know why it was called Egypt, but I think it went far back in history.)

Myself and Roger Young on the left. It's hard to tell because I was always taller than he was.

One big treat I used to experience frequently was to "help" Mr. Jay Gibbs ring the bell in the town clock at noon. It was his job to ring it three times a day, once at 7:00 a.m., once at noon, and once at 9:00 p.m. I'm sure I wasn't all that helpful, but Mr. Gibbs was a very tolerant man. The bell had to be rung the traditional 52 strokes, for what reason there have always been several theories. Stopping it was always a well-timed exercise, and I always wanted to do it. Mr. Gibbs finally relented and said I could, but cautioned me not to hang onto the rope real tightly, or it would take me right up off the floor. I listened closely, but of course I didn't perform the way I was supposed to, and the next thing I knew I was looking down at Mr. Gibbs. Anyway, it was fun, and he was a real nice guy, I always thought.

Opposite our house in Hussey Street lived an elderly couple who quite obviously did not like kids and weren't reluctant to express their displeasure with us. This of course was a big mistake on their part. Their doorbell got pushed more times than most people's. Once we found a rather large wagon wheel—I think it stood at least as high as we did. It took two of us, Clifton Cady and me, to manage the thing. We poised it uphill at the intersection of Quince and Westminster streets, aimed at this elderly couple's steps, and "let her go." It made a wonderful clatter and pounding going up the steps and across the porch to slam into the far wall. Why it didn't break anything, I don't know. Again, we were nowhere to be seen long before the police arrived. We never gave a thought to whether a car might have been coming through Hussey Street—indeed, it would have been even more interesting if there had been one.

In the summertime there would be several older Portuguese gentlemen who picked blueberries out on the moors and then go door-to-door selling them. (Remember, these were Depression days and work was very scarce.) Well, the elderly couple across the street promptly put a small sign on their gate that led to their back door saying "No blueberries, please." The word "No" got mysteriously painted out, and it was fun to watch a small procession of blueberry peddlers going in and out. Mean little kids!

And speaking of mean little kids, a group of us were spending an afternoon at the Jetties Beach, in the area of the channel, to the right of the parking area. We were grade-school age, and one of us

35

discovered a burlap bag, weighted and tied, which immediately aroused our curiosity. On getting it open, we found it contained some live eels, and we had more fun chasing those eels around in the shallow water, until they all got away. It never occurred to us that we had liberated someone's dinner; we were too busy having fun chasing them.

Mr. Irvin Wyer's stable at the northern extremity of Centre Street was one of our favorite hangouts, too. Fortunately for all of us, Mr. Wyer was fond of kids and always very nice to us. There used to be a box of sugar cubes carefully put away in Mr. Wyer Sr.'s old roll-top desk, but we would find it and partake of a few, which were, of course, intended for the horses, not the little brats who wandered in. Mr. Wyer and his father would turn the other way when we thought we were purloining one or two cubes. It was a popular place for the summer folks who liked saddle horses or needed surreys for a special occasion. The main attraction as far as we kids were concerned was the pretty little wicker-sided pony carts. Often a birthday party would include the rental of one of these carts. Mr. Wyer also had huge workhorses for heavy hauling and plowing fields. He would plow the sidewalks after a snowstorm, and rearrange the sand at the beach after the winter winds had drifted it into places where it wasn't wanted, and this involved one horse, one large scoop, and one man.

In the summertime, when we were probably ten or twelve years old, one of our favorite pastimes was to pack a lunch, hop on our bikes, and head for the surf at the Reedy Pond, or Mioxes (on the southwest part of the island), where we would spend the entire day swimming, walking the beach, and sunning without ever seeing another person! The only time the beach crowd is that small these days is in the middle of winter. Of course there were no four-wheel-drive vehicles to be had then. The Jetties Beach and that little bit of public area at Cliffside Beach were also favorite spots. I hardly ever spent any time at the Children's Beach in the harbor—it always struck me as being much too close to "civilization," and I didn't like the orange peels and other debris that would wash ashore there from the boats occupying the harbor.

ON THE WATERFRONT

As a grade-schooler, I spent many hours along the waterfront. There was an old lumber schooner tied up at the west end of the Island Service Company slip, the Ada C. Schull. How I used to love clambering all over that derelict, imagining myself sailing the South Seas or headed for the Grand Banks. There was also a small oil-carrying vessel, the Nantisco, but I don't think it was in the state of disrepair then that the Ada C. Schull was. One of them was towed "up harbor," beached, and set ablaze. That saved a lot of involvement in disposing of it in any other manner.

There were lots of small powerboats tied up in the same slip, and in hanging around there as much as I did, I managed to bum a few rides with the owners. I remember well Joe King's Ethel K., a neatly kept lobster boat, and the Viking, Sam Mathison's dragger. Mr. Yerxa had a small fleet of catboats on which he took picnickers in the summer, and also rented out some small Beetlecats. The other small powerboats in there were used mostly in scallop season, and the predominant power source then was the old single-cylinder engine— a Fairbanks, or maybe a Lycoming—and when it ran it made a continuous loud popping noise. This was in the thirties. On the opening day of commercial scalloping, November 1, the harbor was a cacophony of those powerboats, and they could be heard all over town. Once the engine was started, the boat was under way; there was no clutch or gearshift. To reverse these boats required some expert timing on the part of the operator. A knife switch had to be pulled open at the right moment, and then closed again at also the right

The lumber schooner, Ada C. Schull, tied up at the south side of Island Service Company's Wharf, later at the bulkhead on the other side of the wharf, where I used to scramble all over it.

— *Photo courtesy of the Nantucket Historical Association*

moment. A misstep in the timing resulted in the boat continuing along its path, which had better be clear. I can see it now, an owner laboriously cranking on one of those big lumps of ironwork, blessing it for not firing, and otherwise doubting "modern miracles." Opening the knife switch was also supposed to stop the engine, but sometimes it would be so hot from running that it wouldn't stop when the ignition was shut off. I believe this was known as firing under the heat of compression, much like a Diesel engine. This also brought some interesting results from time to time. It seemed when one refused to fire, nothing in the world would make it go. Then came the Model A Ford engines and other four-cylinder marine engines, all equipped with self-starters and clutches.

Sometimes a local dragger would come in, and more than likely I knew a crewman, who would give me a good-sized codfish, which I proudly took home. My mother was always glad to see that; it was the main course for yet another meal. At that age I wasn't overly fond of fish, but I knew my mother would cook it up into a perfect dinner. Because of that I am now very fond of any seafood. Some of her dinners were quite simple, as far as ingredients go, but oh, so good. There was an old New England recipe she used that called for salt codfish, pork-scrap gravy, and boiled potatoes. Her name for it was "Cape Cod Turkey." There was practically nothing to it, but one could hardly refuse a second helping. Lobster was a luxury we didn't have very often. Now that my son is a commercial lobsterman, we get plenty of it in the summer, but I don't get tired of it.

ROAMING AROUND THE BOATS

During Prohibition it was not uncommon to see a neatly kept fishing boat come and go around Brant Point, much too neat and well painted to be engaged in the dragging business. Once when I was on the milk truck with Frank Powers, his stepfather Ed Gardner, who was driving, stopped briefly at the Children's Beach and laughed at such a boat just leaving the harbor, speaking his opinion about how much fishing they were doing. In those years it was not uncommon to see a Coast Guard boat tied up at the steamship company's wharf, from whence it occasionally left suddenly. We kids got friendly with the crew and were allowed to roam aboard the boat. Their cook made great apple pies, and we were happy to sample them for him and express our approval. None of them were local people, but very nice young men, and despite the Depression years they had a pretty good job, whatever the pay was. These particular Coast Guard boats were known as the "six-bitters," because of the gun mounted on the bow, which fired a shell weighing six pounds. They had little if any other armament on them—maybe some Thompson .45-caliber submachine guns, or .30-caliber machine guns. There were some high-powered craft afloat in those years, high-powered strictly for the purpose of outrunning the Coast Guard. Some of them were quite successful at it, too. I recall the mention of the "Liberty" engines that were popular for that purpose. In our Tuckernuck house I came across a book entitled *The Rum War At Sea*, in which several boats I remember on the Nantucket waterfront were mentioned and pictured.

In those years there were a number of locally owned and crewed fishing boats. We kids were forever going aboard, and were seldom if ever admonished for it. Many of them would keep a pound of butter, in one chunk, on or near the rail. I finally figured out the reason for this: they would dab the dry sounding lead in it before throwing it overboard. The butter would pick up the sand, mud, or gravel, thereby telling the fishermen about what kind of bottom was there, as well as the depth. What was on the bottom of the lead also told them approximately where they were. (Another unique use for butter, as my father told us, was to grease wagon axles; this was during his youth. Butter only cost three cents per pound then.) The other navigational aids on these fishing boats were the compass and clock; there were no radios or electronic aids to navigation of any kind—they didn't exist then. Captains Rolf Sjolund, Olaf Anderson, Jack MacDonald, and Tobias Fleming, among others, were masters at their trade, and could take their vessels to the very spot they had in mind, minus any electronic advantages, for certain. A very few boats were lost at sea, and I have heard it theorized by more than one dragger man that they very well could have been "cut down" by an ocean liner in the middle of the night. A liner could do that, and the crew of the liner would never know they had hit anything. Much the same as a person driving a car and not knowing he had hit a rabbit. Other fishing boats were indeed casualties of very bad weather, and all of us lost friends that way, sadly enough. It is also possible that some got iced up so badly in the rigging, adding a lot of top weight, that they keeled over in a frigid gale. It was a hard way to make a living, even when the fish were more plentiful.

RIDING TO EEL POINT, MILKING COWS, & SOAPING WINDOWS

I was a loner to some extent, and thoroughly enjoyed riding my bike on just about every dirt and rutted road on the island. I would often pack a lunch and make a day of it, except in the wintertime, when it was more convenient to have lunch at home, but I still "lived and died" on that bike. One of my favorite rides in the winter started at the Jetties Beach, at low tide—I would soften the balloon tires just a bit, and ride the beach all the way to Eel Point without stopping. It could be done then. The only small hazard was the little stream that drained out of a small pond, but by getting up some speed I could splash through it. The beach was even better to ride on when it was frozen, because that didn't require softening the tires. My hands were often stiffly removed from the handlebars in cold weather—I wouldn't realize just how cold they were until I got off the bike. Being a real skinny kid, I didn't have a lot to fight the cold air with. That was even more evident when I would be skating, or ice boating on Hummock Pond with my closest boyhood chum, Frank Powers. I used to think that Frank had the greatest life in the world, and it was always a big treat for me to be invited to stay overnight at his house, the old farmhouse that stood on this spot where I live now, 166 Hummock Pond Road. Several of us thought it was great to milk cows in the old cow barn, but we didn't have to do it twice a day, every day, as Frank did. In our high school days I would meet Frank in the morning and the two of us would deliver the milk, then go to school. He was a very hard worker, and was probably the healthiest guy in our class.

Frank would invariably pick me up in Hussey Street and we would deliver it together. His last stop would be the First National Store on Main Street, about where Patten's Jewelry Shop is now. Mr. Brison was the manager of the store, and Frank, knowing that Brison was a little short of temper, liked to antagonize him. One day, Brison was standing right over Frank while he was filling the milk cooler, which didn't please Frank very much, so he "accidentally" dropped a

40

case of full quarts right on Brison's foot, which produced some amusing gymnastics from Mr. Brison. A milk crate in those days was wooden, with metal bindings, and was heavy, especially when full. We were laughing very hard on the way out of the store, and Brison didn't like the fact that I was so amused. He tried to express his displeasure by giving me a swift kick, but I was elusive enough to cause him to kick the door latch instead, which caused him some more discomfort. We weren't too welcome at the First National for awhile.

When we were in high school, Frank Powers and I decided we should have a gunning camp, as my father and Mr. Winslow had on Long Pond. So we built ours on Hummock Pond, on land owned by Frank's family. It wasn't very big, and sported two small windows facing the pond, the door facing east. Two wooden bunks, a table and two chairs, and a small two-burner oil stove on a shelf for cooking comprised the major furnishings of our castle. Because the stove was not vented into a flue, we were severely admonished not to fall asleep with it going, for obvious reasons. One night, both of us being quite tired, we stretched out on our bunks. I was in the top bunk and suggested to Frank that he turn off the oil stove, which he did by just blowing out both burners. This precipitated a very hasty exit for both of us, and the exchange of a few harsh words.

Building this camp was fun, too. My father gave us a number of very large two-inch-thick planks, with which we fashioned a floor and a roof. Not every edifice can lay claim to a roof of two-inch planking. It was nice having the roof that heavy, because that meant we could stand on it and sight up and down the pond. We camouflaged the shack by putting brush and branches on that roof. In fact, it was so well camouflaged that yours truly stepped off the edge of it once, getting to the ground in one big step, somewhat disheveled. I remember well my father and Ed Gardner critiquing our construction by agreeing it was neither "plumb, square, nor level." In spite of those architectural discrepancies, however, it stood for several years.

One morning, very early, and after an all-night northeast blizzard, we had to literally force our way out, as the door was ice coated and sealed shut. It was a long walk up to the farmhouse, and we were not exactly early to milk the cows. Had I realized then that in a very few short years I would be camping in Army tents on the shores of the Bering Strait in winter weather, my enthusiasm for Hummock Pond camping may not have been so intense. Well, even Bering Strait camping had some rewards to it, such as finally leaving the place!

During our high school years, we were only a little politically oriented, but enough to be mischievous about it. The Inquirer and Mirror's office and print shop was located on Orange Street, probably number 1, just a few steps off Main Street. Mr. Harry Turner was the owner, publisher, and editor of the paper in those years, and he wasn't reluctant to take the Democrat party to task for anything and everything. Consequently, one Halloween night, his generous-sized window and door got appropriately decorated with soapy information about voting for Roosevelt, and being the WPA headquarters, etc. This brought the desired results: the very next issue of the Inquirer and Mirror allowed as how the perpetrator of this serious crime should "be horsewhipped," which proved very amusing to said perpetrator. Again, it was not destructive mischief—even so, I kept my mouth shut about it for a while. My father asked me if I knew anything about the incident, and I lied that I didn't, while trying hard not to show a smile. I know he understood very well.

Frank went into the U.S. Marine Corp during the war, and I, with quite some difficulty due to substandard eyesight, finagled my way into the U.S. Army. I had tried several times to enlist in the Navy, but they would have none of it. I actually cheated a little bit on the eye test and finally got into the Army. I'm still not sure I did the right

In the backyard of 19 Hussey Street, left to right—myself, Frank Powers, Arthur Parker, and brother Donald, circa 1935–36.

thing. In retrospect, it seems like time wasted for me, with little or no advantage to Uncle Sam's war effort. To say that Frank's military stint was more interesting and active than mine would be a gross understatement. As an aviation mechanic, he was in the thick of jungle warfare in the South Pacific. He often was obliged to dodge Japanese bullets, and had a very lively time at it. I never heard a shot fired in action, which, with my brand of luck, was probably just as well.

We teamed up again after the war, and worked together for a year or more. We remained the best of friends until his death in 1986. Quite by chance, Mary and I acquired this house that Frank had built on the site of the old farmhouse, when Frank's widow, Donna, decided to go back to her ancestral home in Canada. It affords me some very pleasant boyhood memories, every time I look out a window or walk around the place; it is also nice having Frank, Jr. living right across the road. I don't think Frank Sr. and I could have gotten along better had we been brothers. In fact, anyone who couldn't get along with Frank Powers would have had to be very different indeed, and have had big problems. He was probably one of the most easygoing people one would ever expect to meet, and couldn't possibly have had any enemies. Not many of us can make such a claim.

FUN WITH MY BEST FRIEND

In our school days when either Frank or I had a birthday, we would stay overnight at each other's house. On his birthday I stayed at the farm, which to me was always a big treat. We would go to the duck pond across the road and break out some ice, and Mrs. Gardner would make ice cream; we would have the job of turning the crank on the freezer. Money couldn't buy ice cream as good. Both the ice and the cream were gotten from this location, and we kids supplied the labor.

We skated by the hour on that little duck pond, but as we got a little older we were allowed to skate on Hummock Pond. About this time, Frank's stepfather built an excellent iceboat, which is when I learned how much fun it is to sail. In it, we managed to get from one end of Hummock Pond to the other in no time at all. It was a mighty cold sport, and my skinny physique would get thoroughly chilled very quickly, so I would jump off and skate for a while to build up some body heat. One or two brave souls drove their cars about on the ice—I had a few qualms about doing that, but nobody ever got in trouble doing it, that I remember.

One time, Frank Powers and I and his father and the hired hand went over to Ram Pasture to load the recently-cut hay. I guess we were all of twelve years old. Our job was to stay in the hay wagon and trample the stuff down when they'd heave it up to us with the pitchforks, and stay out of the way of the pitchforks. When we'd get this mountain of hay built, they got in the pickup truck and came back here to the farm leaving us to bring the horse and the hay wagon home. Coming through Mill Brook Road, something happened to the harness, and the horse couldn't move...so one of us had to get down off the heap of hay and put it to rights. I was elected to slide down off the hay wagon—which seemed like a four or five-story building—and put it to rights. I had to walk the rest of the way, because there's no getting back up on the wagon. But that's all right, because the horse didn't move very fast anyway.

They had that horse for many years, and we would coax the poor old plug out of the barn, put a bridle on him, and ride bareback up to the Larrabee Farm and back. Real Wild West! He would never trot, just lope along, but we had fun anyway. One of our number was not very horse-oriented, and didn't know how to control him, and nearly got wiped off when the horse decided he had had enough of us and went back into the barn, unannounced. I think that old horse ended his days in the ownership of Manuel Saunce, who lived on Lower Pleasant Street, where Phillip Marks lived more recently, and always had a huge vegetable garden. I almost cried every time I saw that old horse in his last years, because he had a bad tooth, which swelled up the side of his face and finally burst. It always drained after that, and I could never understand how that poor animal could stand it. It hurt just to look at him.

I think one of the darkest moments of my childhood had to be when my playmate Martin Lamens, more commonly known among us as Leonard, lost his father. When he was a very young man, he died suddenly while out fishing on a dragger. Leonard's mother did a great job of raising Leonard and his older sister, Louise, by herself, and that wasn't easy, because it had to be in the deepest part of the Depression years. At about the same time as his father's death, Leonard's wooden wagon, similar to mine, was misappropriated, and he lamented the fact to me by saying, "Gee, my father died and my wagon got stolen." It struck me as a tragedy bigger than any tragedy, not to mention the two at once. Incidentally, his wagon was found shortly thereafter at the corner of Quince and Centre Streets. About two years later when we had graduated to bicycles, Leonard was riding his down the path at the Sea Cliff Inn and doing some acrobatics on it as he shot out onto North Beach Street, when he suddenly he met one of our school teachers driving her car. He put quite a depression in the grillwork of her car, and was out of school for a couple of days. During World War II he joined the Navy, and his older sister became a nurse in the Army; in later years she was the very popular operating-room nurse in the local hospital.

Working for $3 a Week

One winter in the very early thirties, my father started a delivery service with a resurrected Model-T Ford truck, delivering groceries for the A&P and First National Stores. Later, my summer job was as a helper on one of the Ford station wagons he had by then, and my hours were from 8:00 a.m. to 6:00 p.m., six days a week. My salary was a magnificent $3 per week, which really was pretty good for a ten- or twelve-year-old kid then. The next step in my working career was delivering telegrams for the local Western Union.

Mr. Benson Chase was my boss in the Western Union, and a better boss nobody ever had. I stayed with that job for two or three years, at least. Once, during my high school years, Ben had shown me enough about the teletype machine and other Western Union gadgetry so that I could go to the Main Street office in the early morning, call Boston on the teletype, get all the night letters, record them, and deliver them before going to school. I thought I was quite the hotshot, and worked up somewhat of a rapport with the Boston operator. Well, one morning I seemed to have made contact with a different operator, who for some reason took exception to something I either did or said and was trying to reprimand me for it. However, I would have none of his stuff and told him so in no uncertain terms. The next thing I saw on the tape was a question as to who I was,

45

followed by the initials W.C. Now, W.C. meant Wire Chief, who, in a city telegraph office was next to God himself, and you did not cross one. That much I knew, but I didn't know how to explain myself to the Wire Chief, particularly because I was actually an illicit operator, so I simply pulled the plug and went to school. I sat there all day worrying about whether I had gotten Ben in trouble. Jobs were not all that plentiful in those years, and Ben had a family. Nothing was ever said about it, and I certainly didn't ask any questions about it at the time. But years later I mentioned it to Ben, and he got a big laugh out of it. It had been no laughing matter to me when it happened, and from that time on I was a little more careful and circumspect on the W.U. wire. When I started that job I was getting $12 per week, to me a small fortune. As time went on, you learned who to give the best service to, which always paid off, so for a guy in high school I was doing all right financially. One such summer when I worked for the Western Union I installed a small odometer on my bike and recorded better than 2,000 miles on it. After one mile now, I need a rest!

The infamous 1938 hurricane happened during my stint with Western Union, and the submarine cable parted somewhere west of Madaket. That necessitated the arrival of the ship Cyrus Field, which commenced dragging for the cable within sight of Madaket. Ben and I were obliged to sit for hours wearing a pair of headphones waiting for the call from the ship. I would go down to the office promptly from school and relieve Ben, and of course it was one of those times when they had picked up the cable and called, so I had the big thrill of being the first one to talk with them. I also sat in Gus Bentley's radio shack in his Lily Street home while he handled quite some Western Union traffic using a telegraph key on his ham radio transmitter. This got me hopelessly hooked on radio communications, to the point that when I went into the Army in 1942 I expressed a desire for radio communications, hoping to get some schooling in it. This, of course, immediately got me assigned to the Chemical Warfare branch of Uncle Sam's Army, absolutely the worst and most boring part of his army. After nearly two years of that, I was finally assigned to an engineering construction battalion where I later became the supply sergeant, a job for which I had no experience or training. On arriving at that construction battalion, on the sunny, tropical paradise of Adak in the Aleutian Islands, I noticed on the list of ratings that there was a slot for a "chemical warfare sergeant," and I still think I was probably the only one in the entire battalion that could legitimately qualify for it. But the rating was given to a truck driver, and I never heard any more about the position. That and other kinds of foolishness killed any enthusiasm I might have had for military life.

During high school I worked briefly in Mr. R.G. Coffin's drugstore on the corner of Federal and Main Streets, but the hours he required, and his frugality, persuaded me to go back to the Western Union.

I think it was in my last year of high school that I worked for a short time in Congdon's Pharmacy for Mr. Harry Rex. He and Mr. Fairbanks were very nice people to work for, and they wanted me to stay on through the summer, but I had already promised my grandfather I would drive taxis and tours for him. That job required long hours and seven days a week. It paid the princely sum of $18 weekly, but I made at least that much more in gratuities, and banked most of it. Just what I ever did with "all that money" I don't remember. It certainly wasn't wasted on a motor vehicle, because I never owned one until after my "military career" in World War II, and that was a 1937 Studebaker, a rather tired vehicle.

TOWN CHARACTERS

Town characters? Yes, we had a few, but one has to be careful about discussing them—they just might have descendants among us now. With no offense intended, I can remember "Rolly Ghost" Coffin. He was an old man, I think, when my father was a kid, and I remember my father saying there was probably nobody on the island who could skate better than Rolly Ghost, when indeed there was any ice...and Rolly was sober. I can see him now, wearing a heavy overcoat, summer or winter. We kids did indeed tease him, just to make him chase us. I also remember him telling a couple of unsuspecting tourists that he'd been a captain on one of the island steamers—I had trouble keeping a straight face. Rolly got his nickname from getting drunk and having hallucinations, and calling out to his wife to bring his gun. I do recall his comment once when we harassed him, but I hesitate to put it in print. He almost caught us, we were laughing so hard.

Then there was Willy Collins. Willy was completely harmless, and we never teased him to be mean, but we would ask him to play his "bugle," and he would do a pretty good imitation of one. About the only jobs I remember him doing was errands, or maybe cutting grass somewhere. Mrs. Ditmars, who lived on the west corner of Pleasant and Main Streets, was always very good to Willy, and watched out for him. Willy was still very much around after World War II. Shamefully enough, I never did know when any of our town characters expired.

We also had "Happy Jack"—I never did know his real name. He was almost always pushing a wheelbarrow around, usually with nothing in it. If we greeted him at all, he would answer with "Ah, muh boy" and go limping off on his way. He had a sort of stumbling walk, which helped to make him seem a little different, or maybe a little funny. Jack was still here after the war, too.

And then there were the Burdick brothers, who lived in the house on the west corner of Walnut Lane and Main Street, the house later owned and occupied by Dr. Menges. Walter Burdick was allegedly quite a mathematical genius, but all I ever knew him to do was cut grass. I believe he was a figure in one of the local banks at one time. His brother George was almost blind, wore dark glasses, was very stooped, and wore a dark jacket or overcoat, with a slouched hat pulled well down. He would fish off one of the wharves in the early evening and catch the biggest eels, and often could be seen walking home with one slung over his shoulder.

The gambrel-roofed house in North Liberty Street, opposite Franklin Street, was occupied by the McAnn brothers, Tom and Henry. Tom may have been somewhat of a character and the kids teased him at times, until one fine day he had had too much and took a pitchfork from his ever-present pushcart and threw it at a youngster. After that, we all gave him a wide berth. He obviously knew how to get some peace and quiet. There used to be a lot of pushcarts around in those days, but there was about one one-hundredth of the present-day auto traffic.

Charlie Chase was the official street sweeper, and he handled the entire downtown business district, alone! And that included sweeping the brick sidewalks into the gutters, and then cleaning up the gutters. Now one can see three and four DPW vehicles, and at least a half-dozen men, doing that every summer morning. Progress, you know. Charlie's vehicle was a pushcart equipped with two metal trash barrels, a broom, and a shovel. He swept Main, Federal, Center, South Water, Broad Streets, and areas of Washington, Union, and Orange Streets. It was not unusual for Charlie to have some cold "refreshments" stashed away in his pushcart. I was once told that back in the days when it was legal to dig soft-shelled clams for the market, Charlie would row to Tuckernuck in a dory and dig clams, but he would not go unless he had orders enough to constitute a dory-full. One of his offspring, Richard, entered the U.S. Army along with me and three or four others in December of 1942.

ORGAN-GRINDERS, HURDY-GURDIES, AND HOTDOGS

Summer would bring a lot of different things to the island. Among them were the man with the hand organ and monkey, the two men with the big hurdy-gurdy, and the scissors-grinder. I think they were all Italian men. The organ-grinder frequented the downtown area, and it seemed that we kids all followed him from one stop to another. I can see him now crying out "Mussolini," whereupon the monkey would instantly give the Fascist salute. That idea more than likely faded with the onset of World War II. The two men with the hurdy-gurdy would drag it all over town, making frequent stops to serenade the particular neighborhood. One would crank the machine while the other went to different doorways to encourage a financial handout. I can still see certain of the older people giving them money and suggesting they move on. Not music lovers, obviously. The hurdy-gurdy was a big machine, mounted on two large wheels; it produced rather harsh sounds, always the same tunes of course, and the men really had to pull hard going up any incline.

The scissors-grinder had a little foot-operated machine that he carried slung on his back, and walked along ringing a hand bell. Housewives hearing the bell would come out with their knives and scissors to be sharpened. In more recent years his successor, his son I believe, came better equipped in a van-type motor vehicle.

A more permanent fixture on the island was Professor Jim, the well-known bootblack. His place of business was his fancy one-seat

49

stand, located wherever he could get permission to put it. At one time he did indeed have a very small "storefront" on Middle Pearl Street, across from John Terry's garage. I believe the Gourmet Shop currently occupies the site of John Terry's taxi stand. Later on Professor Jim, whose proper name was Max Doroff, had his stand in front of Rupert Warren's blacksmith shop in South Water Street, close to the rear of the Nobby Shop building's present location. Professor Jim had yet another thriving enterprise—a little metal stand from which he sold hot dogs at night, perhaps on the corner of Federal and Main Streets. How he kept them hot I don't recall, but he did. He didn't have much, if any, competition in those years. We know how much of that would be tolerated today.

The blacksmith shop was yet another spot where one could consume an hour or so, watching Rupert Warren shoe horses, and fashion other strange shapes of iron. The other blacksmith shop of interest was Mr. Cormie's on Straight Wharf, where there would often be an interesting cribbage game going on. Mr. Cormie, who had originally had a partner, Mr. Fred Heighton, was a very quiet gentleman, and very pleasant to do any business with. Among many other items, he made a lot of the dredge frames used in the local scallop fishery. Fishing vessels would get ironwork done by both blacksmith shops.

With our present regulations, laws, rules, and officialdom, those people would probably not be allowed to operate today—especially Professor Jim, with his hotdog-vending enterprise. So much for progress. I wonder if a kid could go door to door selling his own home-grown vegetables, or would modern law prohibit such a young entrepreneur now? Would he have to have perhaps a state seal of sanitation, or have his produce inspected? And pay taxes? We thought our government was getting too big when we were required, even in junior high school, to procure a Social Security card. I certainly don't regret it now, but I do regret that our fearless elected leaders in Washington discovered that Social Security was such a well-endowed administration that they blew the money illicitly, and nothing was ever done about it except to predict that Social Security would soon go broke. One has to wonder about the hundreds of billions that have been paid into it, and it keeps disappearing. All in the interests of progress, of course…

POSTWAR BEACHBUSSING

In the years immediately following World War II, we had a few "characters" who rode our beach buses, in fact, and in retrospect, I think some of them were doing it for amusement. The idea of being in a "laid-back" atmosphere typical of a small resort town seemed to turn them on. At least it tended to liven up an otherwise monotonous day of loading and unloading passengers. I recall one gentleman who always wore dungarees, a short-sleeved shirt and a sailor hat. He pulled a real scene once because the bus didn't leave as soon as he got on; he got real mad, left the bus, and stomped off uptown. I was later told he was a psychiatrist. Well, O.K., I guess psychiatrists must come in all sizes and shapes. My chum, Frank Powers, was driving that bus that particular summer, and I thought he was never going to stop laughing over that incident. A good sense of humor was a big asset in that business. One other "character" wasn't quite so amusing. An attractive young woman, maybe in her early twenties, she was always with another young woman, and every time, without fail, she would have some very unpleasant criticisms to make. When I was driving the bus I tolerated this for quite a few times, but it was obvious she was very serious and was going to persist. Finally, one day she commented that she wished there was a better way to get to and from the beach, and I allowed that there was, particularly in her case. She made the mistake of asking how, and I told her to get her own private broom. This not only served as some quick amusement for the other passengers, but she never bothered me again.

I was not sorry to get out of the beach bus business—it would be a genuine nightmare today, with downtown traffic as it is now. It was a seven-day-a-week job, as long as the sun shone. Two buses were hardly enough to handle the traffic a good part of the time, but at other times one was too many. On a really busy day a driver would spend the entire day at the wheel, stopping and going, drenched with perspiration, and by about 5 o'clock would be ready to strangle the next person who asked a stupid question. It was not unusual for us to carry 1100 or 1200 passengers in a single day; the legal capacity of the buses was 20 and 28, and we were allowed 25 percent as standees. At 9 o'clock the next morning it started all over again. On rare occasions one bus might suffer a breakdown, which put all the traffic on the

51

other driver, so then we would spell each other off. Sometimes, in the very late afternoon, often as late as 6:30 p.m., we would make an extra run to the beach in order to have a swim ourselves...and sure enough, some late passenger would force the door open, get into the bus, and sit there actually blowing the horn, trying to get our attention. This would be long after the regular hours, with the bath houses closed and the beach deserted for the most part. One of the many "pleasures" of dealing with the American public. There had to be a better way to make a living. How my father ever stood it in his physical condition, I'll never know. It might indeed have hastened his demise; he died right after the busy summer of 1943.

Even in the years immediately after World War II, the summer season didn't really get going until July 4th weekend, and at Labor Day it was as though a switch had been thrown, and it all stopped. Our population today, both winter and summer, must certainly be no less than double what it was then. We used to pride ourselves in knowing just about all the streets and lanes, but now there are so many new ones we haven't even heard of, containing many, many new houses (not necessarily "homes," but certainly "houses").

When it comes right down to hard facts, we were a great deal better off on Nantucket than our contemporaries in most cities would have been, in terms of "things to do" for kids our age. Which goes right back to my original contention that Nantucket was a pretty good place to be during the big Depression. What a different ball game it is today. We have a lot of very nice things for today's youth, and we should be thankful. The local football program seems to be very successful, as well as other sports programs that have been incorporated into the school system. The facilities are certainly among the best, and it looks at this writing (December, 1997) as if there will soon be an ice-skating rink.

One of the saddest events I was ever involved in, and this really hurt, was being obliged to be on jury duty (yet again) and seeing four of my former Boy Scouts answering drug charges. I didn't sleep well for several nights. How thankful we can be that drugs were not available when we were of high school age—if they were, we at least weren't aware of it. It's hard to believe that with all the youth programs we have today, drugs will creep in and wreak havoc. Peer pressure, I suppose, and of course money.

MANNERS AND MORALS OF YESTERYEAR

One can't help comparing today with yesteryear, and I'm now thinking of today's youth, and what they get away with. Take school as an example: I see boys sitting in school with their hats on, and I'm told those hats are not removed for flag salutes or prayers (if indeed prayers exist in school anymore), or just out of respect for the teachers or the school. There was a definite dress code enforced all the years I went to school—boys wore neckties and girls were dressed like girls and acted like them. No student ever talked back to a teacher without prompt physical attention, most of it not very gentle. Today, if a teacher finally loses his or her temper and swats a student, he or she gets suspended, possibly fired, or sued, or all of the above. I sat at a table at our Rotary lunch one day, with a friend and his fourteen-year-old son whose hat did not come off during our flag salute and prayer. I was sorely tempted to remove it for him, but to retain a friendship, I did not. I did ask him, though, if they do that in school, and he assured me they do. So much for common respect.

Promiscuity was certainly frowned upon in those years. If a woman walked down the street improperly clothed in the opinion of Chief of Police Gibbs, she was ordered off the street and warned that she would be locked up if she didn't comply. And there were others whom the Chief, or the District Court Judge, would admonish to be on "the next boat leaving." The movies were censored in Hollywood where they were made, there was no sleaze on the radio, and certain magazines were forbidden to youngsters (even though of course some of them leaked through). And common crime on Nantucket was the exception, not an everyday happening. On many Superior Court sessions, the Sheriff would hand the judge a pair of white gloves, symbolic of there being no criminal cases on the docket. Impossible today!

There was a State Police contingency on the island in those years, which was probably started during prohibition. Although I was a grade-schooler then, I clearly remember hearing of the State Police making arrests, such as the time a planeload of bootleg booze landed somewhere in Surfside and was met by those uniformed people. There are still some interesting stories to be heard. I was told of how booze was secreted in No Bottom Pond, with buoys just below the surface

53

to allow for the relocation, and also heard stories of it being buried in the old fairgrounds, where the Nantucket Electric Company now resides. And a lot of the booze just cruised around in different vehicles, and was sold by the bottle. My father good-naturedly teased one particular party about this, and when he went back to his vehicle there were two very nice bottles on his front seat. They were around the house for many years, because my parents never drank.

Many people brewed beer at home for their own consumption, and others produced it for illicit sale. I remember some of it being called "needle beer," and I think I know why. Others made "bathtub gin," I presume for profit, too. I never saw any of either, I just heard about them. The closest my family came to that was my father making root beer for us. I was well along in high school before I even saw a dinner wine on our table, and then only at Thanksgiving or Christmas. As a younger married man, I had a go at making "home brew," some of which blew up, some of which was quite good.

In concluding my boyhood memories (not all boyhood, obviously), I have to say again and again that there couldn't have been a better place to live out one's boyhood than on Nantucket. Even now (2002), it strikes me that there is ever so much more for youngsters in this town to hold their interests and keep them occupied. All to the good, what with the hazards that befall today's youth—drugs, booze, peer pressure, and so on. We have a sailing program in the summer that is within reach of the average-income parents, and terrific facilities for just about all sports in our school system. The town is much bigger now, our year-round population being 9000, at least, as compared to 3500 fifty and more years ago.

Left to right—my son Warren Pease, myself, and my brother-in-law Byron Coffin, after loading somebody's catboat aboard my trailer.

— *Photo courtesy of the Nantucket Historical Association*

Perhaps many childhoods end on a rather sad note, and mine was no exception. I remember leaving Nantucket to go to Hartford, Connecticut, to work; Bob Henderson, a classmate, was on the same boat with me. I think it was the last time he ever saw Nantucket, and the last time I ever saw Bob, as he became a Marine and was killed in the battle of Guadalcanal about a year and half later. World War II played havoc with our class membership, for at least three others who were in our high school class at one time or another also were lost in World War II.

At any rate, it was great to grow up here, and at age 80, I am still "growing up on Nantucket."

Made in the USA